ALL FORMULAS OF PHYSICS.

BY ALPHA BOOKS.

FAIZ-UL-ISLAM &
NOUMAAN ASHRAF.

Made with ❤ on the Notion Press Platform
www.notionpress.com

THANKS

i) FAIZAN ASHRAF FOR HELPING US IN MAKING THIS BOOK.

ii) NOTION PRESS FOR MAKING THE PUBLICATION OF THIS BOOK POSSIBLE.

iii) YOU . THANKYOU FOR PURCHASING THIS BOOK.

Contents

Preface

HI MY NAME IS FAIZ FAYAZ . I AM THE AUTHOR OF THIS BOOK . ONE DAY I WAS SOLVING SOME PROBLEMS OF PHYYSICS , FOR EVERY QUESTION I HAD TO TURN THE PAGE OF THE BOOK AND LOOK FOR THE FORMULAS . I THOUGHT THAT THERE MUST BE A SOLUTION FOR THIS SO I AND MY FRIEND DECIDED TO WRITE THIS BOOK WHICH CONTAINED ALL THE FORMULAS OF PHYSICS. THAT IS HOW THIS BOOK WAS MADE.

THANKYOU.

ONE

MOTION.

1. Speed (SCALAR)

SPEED = DISTANCE / TIME.

V = S/T

Here,

V = Speed , S = Distance , T = Time.

UNIT OF SPEED = m/s

2. VELOCITY (VECTOR)

VELOCITY = DISPLACEMENT / TIME.

$v \rightarrow = S \rightarrow / T$

Here,

$v \rightarrow$ = Velocity , $S \rightarrow$ = D = Displacement , T = Time.

UNIT OF VELOCITY = m/s

3. AVERAGE

VELOCITY = INITIAL VELOCITY + FINAL VELOCITY / 2

$V \rightarrow av = u + v / 2$

Here,

$v \rightarrow av$ = Average velocity , u = initial velocity , v = final velocity.

SPEED = Total distance / total time taken

Vav = s/t

Here,

Vav = Average speed , S = distance , t = time

ACCELERATION (VECTOR)

Acceleration = Change in velocity / time taken

a = v - u / t

Here,

a = Acceleration , v = final velocity , u = initial velocity.

TWO

SOME DERIVED FORMULAS.

S = V * T

Here,

S = DISTANCE , V = SPEED , T = TIME , * = MULTIPLIED BY

S▸ = V▸ * T

Here,

S → = DISPLACEMENT . V → = VELOCITY , T = TIME

THREE

UNITS OF QUANTITIES LEARNED TILL NOW.

SPEED (V) = m/s

VELOCITY (V▸) = m/s

TIME (T) = second (s)

DISTANCE (S) = m (metre)

DISPLACEMENT (S▸) = m (metre)

ACCELETRATION (a) = m/s ^ 2

FOUR

ALL FORMULAS OF PHYSICS. VOL(II)

$V = u + at$

Here,

V= final velocity , u = initial velocity , t = time

$S\vec{} = ut + 1/2\ at ^ 2$

Here ,

S→ = displacement , u = initial velocity , t = time , a = acceleration

$V^2 - U^2 = 2as$

Here,

V= final velocity , u = initial velocity , a = acceleration , s = displcement

ᑭᑭᑭ

FORCE

FORCE (VECTOR)

FORCE = MASS * ACCELERATION

F = ma

Here,

F = force , m = mass , a = acceletarion.

MOMENTUM (VECTOR)

MOMENTUM = MASS * VELOCITY

P = mv

Here,

P = momentum , m = mass , v = velocity

GRAVITATIONAL FORCE (VECTOR)

Gravitational force = G M1 * M2 / R^2

$F = G\ m1\ m2 / R^2$

Here,

F = Gravitational force , G = Universal gravitational constant ($6.673 \times 10^{-11}\ N\ m^2/kg^2$) , m1 = mass of object 1 , m2 = mass of object 2 , R = distance between the centers of these objects.

KEPLERS LAW OF PLANETARY MOTION.

$R^3 \propto T^3$, R^3/T^3 = CONSTANT.

Here,

R = distance between sun and planet , t = time taken for comleteting one revolution

ACCELERATION DUE TO GRAVITATION.

ACCELERATION DUE TO GRAVITATION = $G\ m / R^2$

$g = GM/R^2$

Here,

g = ACCELERATION DUE TO GRAVITATION , G = universal gravitational constant , m = mass of earth , R = radius of earth.

HINT.

$G = 6.673 \times 10^{-11}\ N\ m^2/kg^2$.

g = 9.8 on earth.

WEIGHT.

WEIGHT = MASS * GRAVITATION

$W = mg$

Here,

W= Weight , m= mass , g = acceleration due to gravity.

PRESSURE.

PRESSURE = FORCE/ AREA

P = FA

Here,

P = PRESSURE , F = FORCE , A = AREA

BUOYANT FORCE.

BUOYANT FORCE = VOLUME * FLUID DENSITY * ACCELERATION DUE TO GRAVITATION (9.8 m/s^2)

Fb = ρgV

Here,

Fb = BUOYANT FORCE , ρ = FLUID DENSITY (Rho) , V = Volume

WORK.

WORK = FORCE * DISPLACEMENT

W = FS

Here,

W = WORK , F = FORCE , S = DISPLACEMENT

KINETIC ENERGY.

KINETIC ENERGY = HALF OF MASS * VELOCITY SQUARED

Ek = 1/2 mv^2

Here,

Ek = KINETIC ENERGY , m = mass , v = velocity

POTENTIAL ENERGY.

POTENTIAL ENERGY = MASS * ACCELERATION DUE TO GRAVITY * HEIGHT

Ep = mgh

Here,

Ep = POTENTIAL ENERGY , m = MASS , g = ACCELERATION DUE TO GRAVITY (9.8 m/s^2)

ENERGY.

1.) ENERGY = MASS * SPEED OF LIGHT SQUARED

E = mc^2

2.) ENERGY = WORK

POWER.

POWER = WORK DONE DEVIDED BY TIME TAKEN.

P = w/t

Here,

P = POWER , w = WORK , t = TIME

UNITS.

FORCE = NEWTON (KG/m/s^2)

MOMENTUM = Newton-second

PRESSURE = PASCAL (N/m^2)

WEIGHT = NEWTON (BECAUSE IT IS A FORCE)

WORK = JOULE (Nm)

ENERGY = JOULE

POWER = WATT (j/s)

FIVE
CLASS 10TH FORMULAS

(1) Mirror formula,

$1/v + 1/u = 1/f$.

(2) Lens formula

$1/v - 1/u = 1/f$.

(3) Electric Current.

Electric Current = charge / time

$I = q/t$.

Here,
I = **Electric Current**, q = charge , t = time

(4) Potential difference.

Potential difference = work done / charge

v = W/Q.

Here,

v = **Potential difference**, w = work done , Q = charge

(5) Ohm's law.

Potential difference = current * Resistance

V = IR.

Here,

V = **Potential difference , I = current , R = Resistance**

(6) Resistivity.

Resistivity = Resistance*Area/Length

ρ = RA/L.

Here,

ρ = Resistivity , R = Resistance , A = Area of wire , L = length of wire

(7) Electric power,

P = W/t = VI = I2R.

PPP

FOCUS

FOCUS = R/2

Here,

R = RADIUS

POWER OF LENS

POWER = 1/ F

Here,

F = Focal Length

MAGNIFICATION

i) M = V/U

Here,

M = Magnification , V = size of image , U = size of object

II) M = Hi / Ho

Here,

Hi = Height of image , Ho = height of object.

REFRACTIVE INDEX OF A MEDIUM.

REFRACTIVE INDEX OF A MEDIUM = SPEED OF LIGHT IN VACUMM / SPEED OF LIGHT IN MEDIUM

$\mu = c/v$

Here,

μ = REFRACTIVE INDEX OF A MEDIUM (mu) , c = speed of light in vacumm , v = speed of light in medium.

RESISTANCE IN SERIES.

RESISTANCE IN SERIES = RESISTOR 1 + RESISTOR 2 (SO ON)

Reff = R1 + R2 + R3 + ...

Here,

Reff = Effective resistance , R1 = Resistor 1 and so on.

RESISTANCE IN PARALLEL.

RESISTANCE IN PARALLEL = 1 / effective reistance => 1 / Resistor 1 + 1 / Resistor 2 and so on.

RIP = 1 / R 1 + 1 / R2 + ...

Here,

RIP = RESISTANCE IN PARALLEL , R1 = resistor 1 and so on.

JOULE'S LAW OF HEATING.

HEAT = CURRENT SQUARED * RESISTANCE * TIME

H = I^2 RT

Here,

H = HEAT , I = CURRENT , R = RESISTANCE , T = TIME.

Important Info.

THANKS FOR BUYING THIS BOOK.

IF YOU NEED MORE INFORMATION HERE ARE OUR SOCIAL MEDIA LINKS.

?WEBSITE LINK :- infoalphabooks.blogspot.com

?EMAIL :- Information.Alphabooks@gmail.com

THANK YOU.

Printed by Libri Plureos GmbH in Hamburg,
Germany